A JOURNAL OF MEMORIES

For All Of Eternity

21 Time Capsules
to Keep Forever

Preserving moments that matter

Why This Book Exists

Life moves quickly. Moments that feel monumental fade into memory, and memories soften with time. This book exists to freeze moments in time before they slip away.

These 21 time capsules are more than prompts—they're an invitation to pause and reflect on the moments, people, and truths that have shaped who you are. They're a way to hold onto the extraordinary hidden within the ordinary.

In filling these pages, you're creating something precious: a record of your heart, your journey, and your wisdom. A gift for those you love—so they can truly know you, understand your story, and cherish the moments that mattered most.

This is your legacy. These are your truths. Preserved for all of eternity.

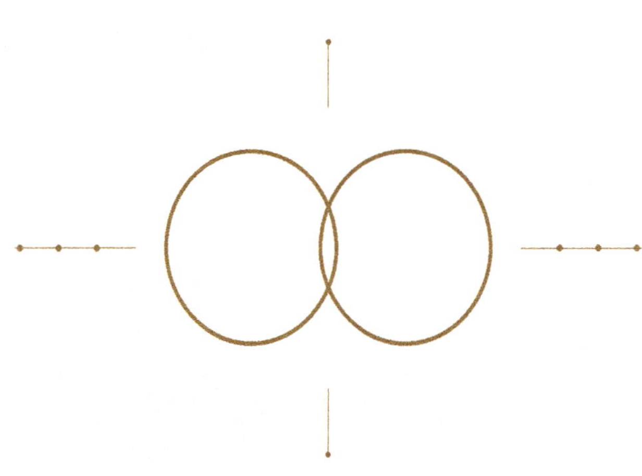

How This Book Works

Each page is a time capsule.

Open to one. Fill it when the moment feels right.

Date it. Seal it with your truth.

Then close the book.

This isn't meant to be read all at once.

Some pages are for today.

Some are meant for later.

Some for much, much later.

This book is meant to live with you—

not be rushed, not be finished.

Let it unfold slowly, one truth at a time.

What we remember becomes
who we are.

For all of eternity

This Time Capsule Belongs To

Given to by

Date received

For all of eternity

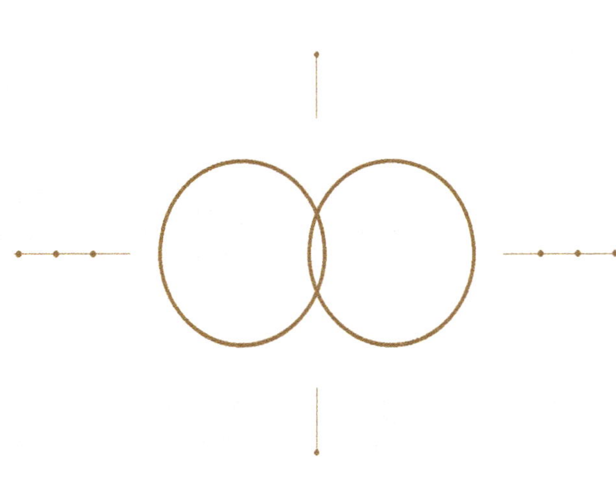

#1

Sealed on: _______________________

A truth I want preserved forever is...

#2

Sealed on: _______________________

The moment I felt most alive was...

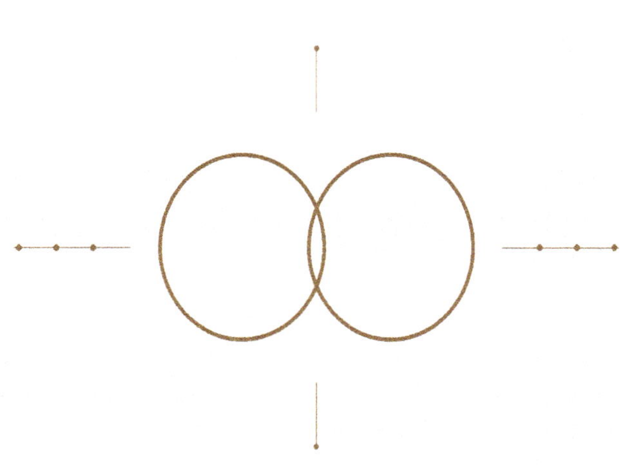

#3

Sealed on: ________________

A person who changed the course of my life...

#4

Sealed on: ___________________

The bravest thing I ever did was...

For all of eternity.

*Love lives on
in what we choose to remember.*

For all of eternity

#5

Sealed on: ___________________

A dream that still calls to me is...

#6

Sealed on: ________________________

The lesson that transformed everything for me...

#7

Sealed on: _____________________

A place that will forever hold a piece of my heart...

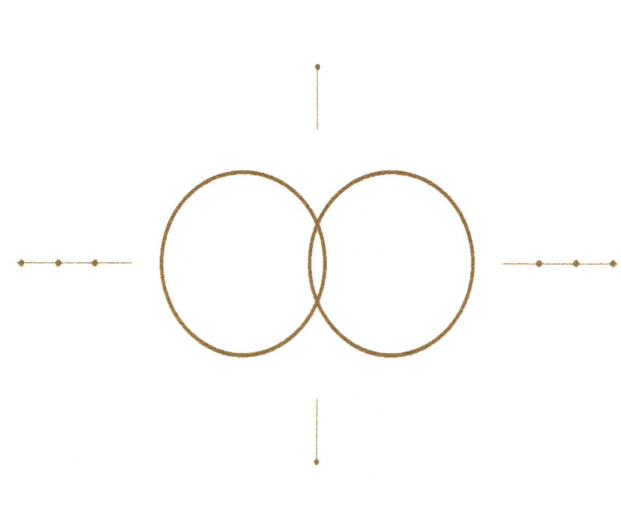

#8

Sealed on: _______________________

The hardest goodbye I ever said was to...

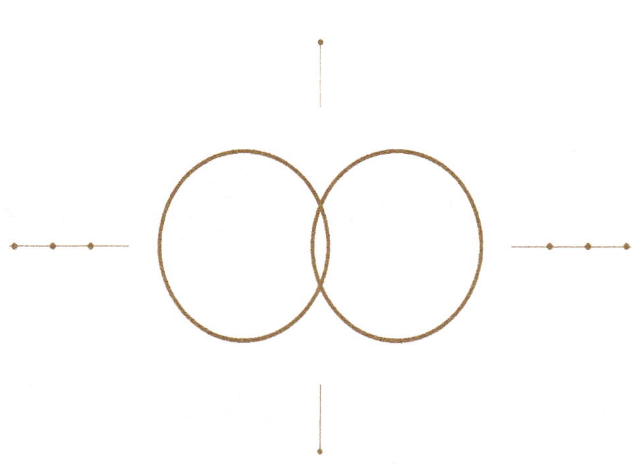

#9

____

Sealed on: ___________________

What I want my younger self to know is...

For all of eternity.

*The heart remembers
what the mind forgets.*

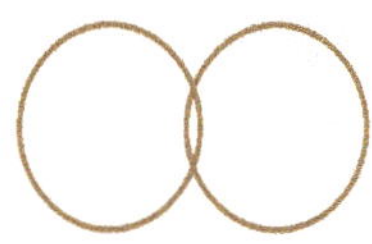

For all of eternity

#10

Sealed on: ___________________

The love that shaped me most deeply...

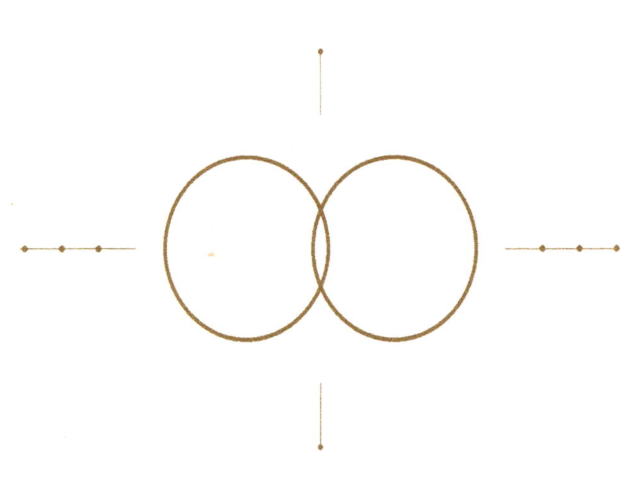

#11

Sealed on: _______________________

A belief I'll carry with me always...

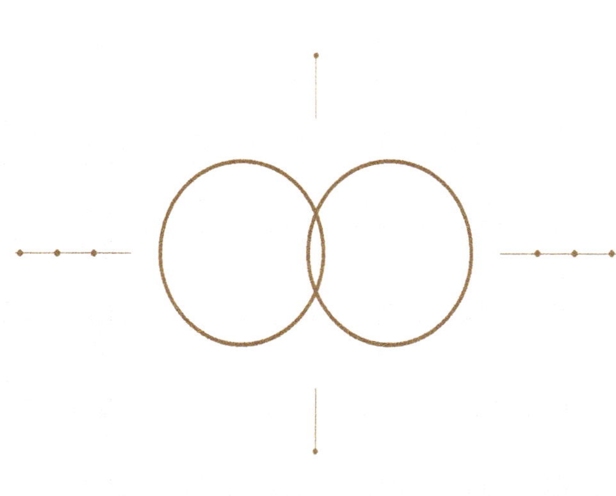

#12

Sealed on: ______________________

The day everything changed was when...

For all of eternity.

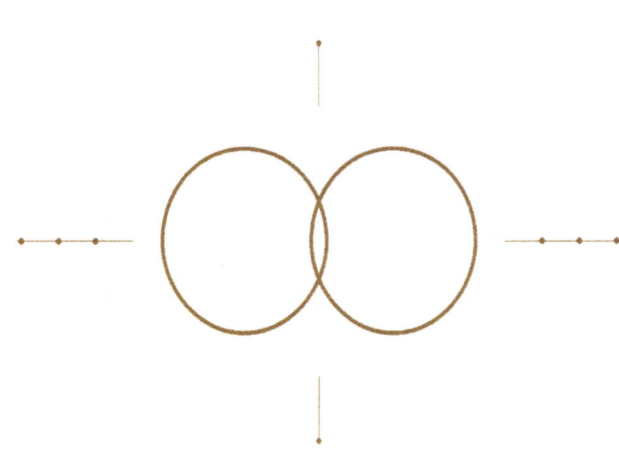

#13

Sealed on: _______________________

Something beautiful I witnessed that no one else saw...

For all of eternity.

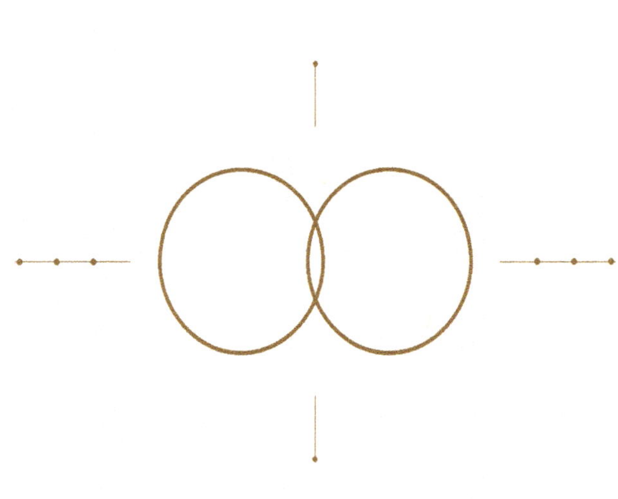

#14

Sealed on: _____________________

A promise I made to myself that I kept...

These moments, these words—
they are your forever.

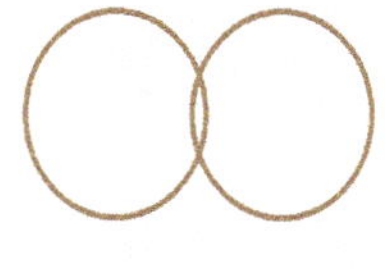

For all of eternity

#15

Sealed on: ___________________

The greatest gift I was ever given was...

For all of eternity.

#16

Sealed on: ___________________

A joy I hope to never forget is...

#17

Sealed on: ________________________

What I've learned about resilience is...

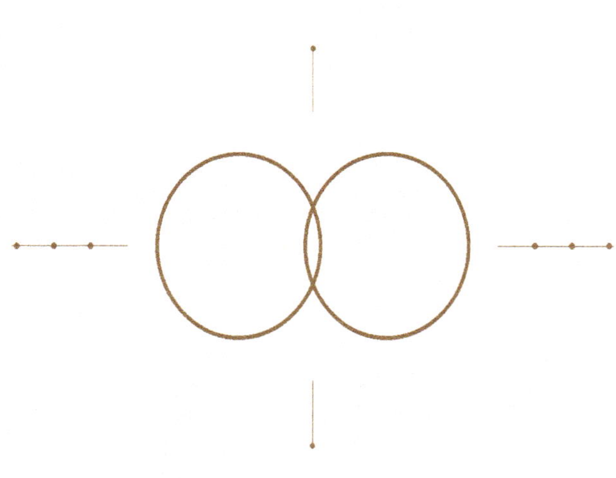

#18

Sealed on: ___________________

The conversation that altered my perspective forever...

For all of eternity.

#19

Sealed on: ______________________

A moment of grace I experienced was...

In preserving our stories,
we honor our truth.

For all of eternity

#20

Sealed on: ___________________

What I want future generations to know about me...

For all of eternity.

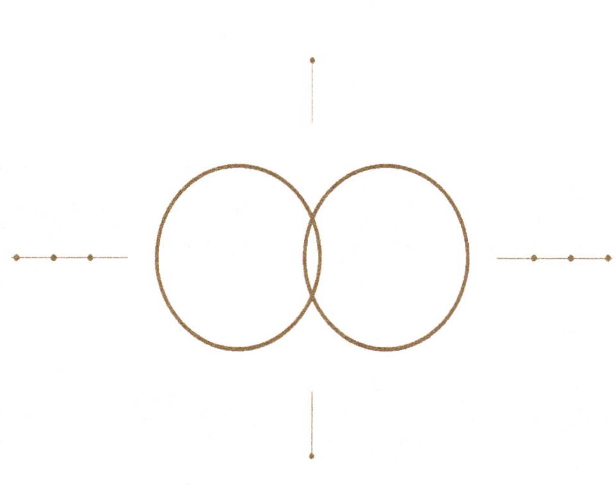

#21

Sealed on: ___________________

*If I could preserve one feeling forever,
it would be...*